Living With Schizophrenia

DR. LIAM SANDERS

COPYRIGHT

TABLE OF CONTENTS

Chapter 1

Understanding Schizophrenia and Schizoaffective Disorder

Introduction

Imagine waking up one day and realizing that the world around you feels different—voices whisper when no one is there, familiar places seem unfamiliar, and your emotions shift unpredictably. For many people living with schizophrenia or schizoaffective disorder, this is their reality.

Schizophrenia and schizoaffective disorder are serious, lifelong mental health conditions that can be deeply misunderstood. While often portrayed in the media as dangerous or hopeless, the truth is that many people with these disorders live fulfilling, meaningful lives—especially with proper treatment and support. This chapter will provide a foundational understanding of both conditions, breaking down common myths, symptoms, and the ways they impact daily life.

What is Schizophrenia?

Schizophrenia is a chronic brain disorder that affects how a person thinks, feels, and behaves. It typically appears in late adolescence or early adulthood and is characterized by episodes of psychosis—periods where a person loses touch with reality.

Core Symptoms of Schizophrenia

Schizophrenia symptoms are often categorized into three main groups:

1. Positive Symptoms (Additions to Reality)

Hallucinations (hearing voices, seeing things that aren't there)

Delusions (false beliefs, such as thinking one is being controlled by aliens)

Disorganized thinking (jumping from topic to topic, incoherent speech)

2. Negative Symptoms (Loss of Normal Functioning)

Social withdrawal and isolation

Lack of motivation or energy

Diminished emotional expression (flat affect)

3. Cognitive Symptoms (Thinking and Memory Issues)

Trouble focusing or making decisions

Poor memory and difficulty organizing thoughts

Difficulty understanding social cues

Not everyone with schizophrenia experiences all these symptoms, and their severity can vary over time.

What is Schizoaffective Disorder?

Schizoaffective disorder is a complex mental illness that combines symptoms of schizophrenia with mood disorder symptoms (either bipolar disorder or major depression). This means someone with schizoaffective disorder not only experiences psychosis (like schizophrenia) but also severe mood disturbances.

Types of Schizoaffective Disorder

1. Bipolar type: Includes both mania (high energy, impulsivity) and depression.

2. Depressive type: Features only major depressive episodes alongside schizophrenia symptoms.

Key Differences Between Schizophrenia and Schizoaffective Disorder

While both conditions require antipsychotic medications, schizoaffective disorder is often treated with additional mood-stabilizing medications to address bipolar or depressive symptoms.

Common Myths and Misconceptions

There's a lot of misinformation about schizophrenia and schizoaffective disorder. Let's clear up some of the most common myths:

1. Myth: People with schizophrenia are violent.

Reality: The vast majority of people with schizophrenia are not violent. In fact, they are more likely to be victims of violence due to social stigma and vulnerability.

2. Myth: Schizophrenia means having "multiple personalities."

Reality: Schizophrenia is not the same as Dissociative Identity Disorder (DID). People with schizophrenia do not have multiple personalities; they experience hallucinations, delusions, and cognitive difficulties.

3. Myth: Schizophrenia cannot be treated.

Reality: While schizophrenia is a chronic condition, many people recover with proper treatment, medication, therapy, and social support. Some even lead completely independent lives.

4. Myth: Schizophrenia is rare.

Reality: It affects about 1 in 100 people worldwide. Schizoaffective disorder is less common but still affects 0.3% of the population.

Real-Life Case Study: Alex's Story

Alex was a 22-year-old college student when he started hearing whispers in the library. At first, he ignored them, thinking they were just his imagination. But as the weeks went on, the voices became louder and more hostile. He started believing his professors were inserting thoughts into his head.

His friends noticed he was withdrawing from conversations, staring off into space, and struggling to keep up with assignments. When he confided in his older sister, she encouraged him to see a psychiatrist. After a thorough evaluation, he was diagnosed with schizoaffective disorder, bipolar type.

With the right combination of antipsychotic medication, therapy, and a strong support system, Alex was able to stabilize his symptoms. He still has challenges, but today, he works part-time as a graphic designer and advocates for mental health awareness.

How Schizophrenia and Schizoaffective Disorder Affect Daily Life

These conditions can impact every aspect of life, from work to relationships. Here's what people with schizophrenia or schizoaffective disorder often struggle with:

Social interactions: Difficulty reading social cues, leading to isolation.

Employment: Jobs with high stress or unpredictable schedules can be overwhelming.

Personal hygiene: Negative symptoms can make self-care hard to maintain.

Medication adherence: Side effects like weight gain, drowsiness, and tremors can make it tough to stick to treatment.

Despite these challenges, many people with schizophrenia and schizoaffective disorder lead meaningful lives when given proper support and accommodations.

Conclusion: The Importance of Understanding and Compassion

Schizophrenia and schizoaffective disorder are not just clinical conditions; they are human experiences that deserve empathy and support. Understanding what these illnesses truly are—and what they are not—is the first step toward breaking the stigma and helping those affected live their best lives.

In the next chapter, we'll dive deeper into the causes and risk factors of these disorders, exploring the complex interplay of genetics, environment, and brain chemistry.

Reflection Questions for Caregivers and Loved Ones

1. Have you ever encountered stereotypes about schizophrenia? How has your perception changed?

2. What are some ways you can help a loved one with schizophrenia or schizoaffective disorder feel supported?

3. If you or someone you love is struggling with symptoms, what steps can you take to seek professional help?

Chapter 2

The Causes and Risk Factors of Schizophrenia and Schizoaffective Disorder

Introduction

Mental health disorders like schizophrenia and schizoaffective disorder don't arise out of nowhere. They result from a complex interplay of genetics, brain chemistry, environment, and life experiences. While researchers don't fully understand why some people develop these conditions while others don't, we do know certain risk factors increase the likelihood.

This chapter will explore what we currently know about the causes of schizophrenia and schizoaffective disorder, breaking it down into biological, environmental, and social influences.

Genetic Factors: The Role of Family History

Schizophrenia and schizoaffective disorder tend to run in families, suggesting a strong genetic component.

If a parent or sibling has schizophrenia, the risk of developing it is about 10%.

If an identical twin has schizophrenia, the other twin has a 50% chance of developing it.

If there is no family history, the general population risk is about 1%.

However, genes alone don't determine who develops the disorder. Many people with a family history never experience symptoms, while others with no family history do. This suggests that genetics increase vulnerability, but environmental factors likely trigger the condition.

Real-Life Example: The Siblings' Story

Elena and her younger brother Marco grew up in the same home. Their father had schizophrenia, and their mother did not. At 22, Marco developed symptoms of schizophrenia, while Elena never did. Why?

Scientists believe a combination of stress, life experiences, and genetic differences led to Marco developing the disorder while Elena remained unaffected. This highlights the importance of both genetic and environmental factors in mental illness.

Brain Chemistry and Structure: The Biological Basis

Brain scans of people with schizophrenia and schizoaffective disorder reveal structural and chemical differences compared to neurotypical individuals.

Neurotransmitter Imbalances

Neurotransmitters are chemicals in the brain that control mood, thinking, and perception. In schizophrenia and schizoaffective disorder, two key neurotransmitters are often out of balance:

1. Dopamine (the "reward" chemical)

Too much dopamine activity in certain brain areas is linked to hallucinations and delusions.

Many antipsychotic medications work by blocking dopamine receptors to reduce psychosis.

2. Glutamate (the "learning" chemical)

Some research suggests low glutamate function contributes to schizophrenia symptoms.

This may explain cognitive issues like difficulty focusing and remembering things.

Brain Structure Differences

MRI studies have found that some people with schizophrenia and schizoaffective disorder have:

Smaller brain volume in certain areas (like the prefrontal cortex, which controls decision-making).

Enlarged ventricles, which may indicate less brain tissue in key regions.

Weaker connections between different parts of the brain, affecting thought processes.

These structural changes may develop before symptoms appear, making early detection difficult.

Environmental Triggers: The Role of Life Experiences

Even with genetic and biological risks, schizophrenia and schizoaffective disorder are often triggered by life events. Some key environmental factors include:

1. Prenatal and Birth Complications

Exposure to viruses (like the flu) during pregnancy.

Oxygen deprivation at birth.

Low birth weight or premature delivery.

These factors can affect brain development and increase schizophrenia risk later in life.

2. Childhood Trauma and Neglect

Physical, emotional, or sexual abuse.

Severe neglect or growing up in an unstable home.

Losing a parent at a young age.

Studies show people with schizophrenia are more likely to have experienced early trauma than those without it.

3. Drug Use (Cannabis, LSD, Methamphetamine, etc.)

Heavy cannabis use during adolescence (especially high-THC strains) can increase schizophrenia risk, particularly in genetically vulnerable individuals.

Psychedelics and stimulants (like LSD, MDMA, and meth) can trigger psychotic symptoms, sometimes leading to long-term schizophrenia-like conditions.

Methamphetamine-induced psychosis can mimic schizophrenia and, in some cases, become permanent.

Important note: Drug use doesn't "cause" schizophrenia, but in people with a genetic predisposition, it can trigger or worsen symptoms.

4. Social Isolation and Stress

Loneliness and lack of social support can worsen symptoms.

High-stress environments, such as living in poverty or experiencing discrimination, can contribute to mental health decline.

Schizoaffective Disorder: Why Are Mood Symptoms Involved?

Schizoaffective disorder is unique because it combines psychosis and mood symptoms. Researchers believe this could be due to:

1. A mix of genetic factors that predispose individuals to both schizophrenia and mood disorders.

2. Dysfunction in serotonin and dopamine systems, affecting both mood and perception.

3. Life events triggering mood instability that interacts with underlying psychotic tendencies.

Unlike schizophrenia, schizoaffective disorder often requires a dual approach to treatment—both antipsychotics and mood stabilizers.

The "Two-Hit" Hypothesis: Why Some People Develop Symptoms and Others Don't

One of the leading theories in schizophrenia research is the "two-hit" hypothesis:

First hit (genetic predisposition): A person is born with a vulnerability due to genetics or prenatal factors.

Second hit (environmental trigger): Stress, trauma, or drug use triggers the onset of symptoms.

This explains why some people with schizophrenia never show symptoms until a major life event (like stress or drug use) activates it.

Real-Life Case Study: Noah's Journey

Noah grew up in a stable home but had a family history of mental illness. In his late teens, he experimented with high-potency cannabis daily. By 20, he began experiencing paranoia and hearing voices. At first, he dismissed it as stress. But when he started believing his family was plotting against him, he was hospitalized and diagnosed with schizophrenia.

His doctors believe that genetics + cannabis use + high stress contributed to his illness. Today, with medication and therapy, he has regained stability and works as a peer support specialist.

Conclusion: A Multifactorial Illness

Schizophrenia and schizoaffective disorder don't have a single cause. They are the result of a complex mix of genetics, brain chemistry, environmental stressors, and life experiences.

Understanding the causes helps us move beyond stigma and see these conditions for what they truly are: brain disorders that require medical support, not personal failures.

Key Takeaways

Genetics play a significant role, but they do not guarantee someone will develop schizophrenia.
 Brain chemistry and structure differences contribute to symptoms.
 Trauma, drug use, and social stressors can act as triggers.
 The "two-hit" hypothesis explains why symptoms may appear later in life.
Early detection and intervention can reduce the severity of symptoms.

In the next chapter, we'll explore how schizophrenia and schizoaffective disorder are diagnosed and the treatment options available.

Reflection Questions for Readers

1. Do you know anyone with a family history of schizophrenia or schizoaffective disorder?

2. How can learning about the causes of these disorders help reduce stigma?

3. What environmental factors do you think should be addressed to help prevent mental illness?

Chapter 3

Diagnosis and Treatment Options for Schizophrenia and Schizoaffective Disorder

Introduction

Schizophrenia and schizoaffective disorder can be difficult to diagnose, especially in the early stages. Symptoms often overlap with other mental health conditions, such as bipolar disorder, depression, and even substance-induced psychosis. However, early diagnosis is crucial for better long-term outcomes.

This chapter will cover how these disorders are diagnosed, common challenges in the diagnostic process, and the treatment options available, including medications, therapy, lifestyle changes, and alternative approaches.

Diagnosing Schizophrenia and Schizoaffective Disorder

The Diagnostic Process

Diagnosing schizophrenia or schizoaffective disorder involves multiple steps and typically requires assessment by a psychiatrist or clinical psychologist.

1. Clinical Interview

The doctor will ask about symptoms, medical history, and family history of mental illness.

They will explore thoughts, behaviors, emotions, and any experiences with hallucinations or delusions.

2. Diagnostic Criteria (DSM-5)

Schizophrenia diagnosis requires at least two of the following symptoms for at least one month, with signs of disturbance for at least six months:

Delusions

Hallucinations

Disorganized speech

Disorganized or catatonic behavior

Negative symptoms (e.g., lack of emotion, motivation, or speech)

Symptoms must cause significant impairment in daily life.

Schizoaffective disorder diagnosis requires:

Schizophrenia symptoms plus mood symptoms (depression or mania).

Mood symptoms must be present for the majority of the illness.

Psychotic symptoms must occur even when mood symptoms are not present.

3. Ruling Out Other Conditions

Substance-induced psychosis (from drugs like meth, LSD, or high-THC cannabis).
Bipolar disorder (if psychosis only happens during mood episodes).

Severe depression with psychotic features.

Neurological disorders (such as epilepsy, brain tumors, or dementia).

4. Medical Tests (When Necessary)

Blood tests (to check for infections or drug use).

Brain scans (MRI or CT scan) (to rule out tumors or structural issues).

Challenges in Diagnosis

Early symptoms (like withdrawal, paranoia, and mood swings) can be mistaken for depression or anxiety.

Many people hide their symptoms out of fear of being judged.

Schizoaffective disorder is often misdiagnosed as bipolar disorder or major depression with psychotic features.

Some patients reject their diagnosis due to anosognosia (a lack of insight into their illness).

Treatment Options

1. Medication: The Foundation of Treatment

Most people with schizophrenia and schizoaffective disorder require medication to manage symptoms.

Antipsychotic Medications

Antipsychotics help reduce hallucinations, delusions, and disorganized thinking by balancing brain chemicals (especially dopamine).

Two main types:

First-generation (typical) antipsychotics (e.g., Haloperidol, Chlorpromazine)

Effective but more likely to cause movement-related side effects (tremors, stiffness).

Second-generation (atypical) antipsychotics (e.g., Risperidone, Olanzapine, Clozapine)

Fewer movement-related side effects but can cause weight gain and metabolic issues.

Clozapine: The "Last Resort" Drug

Used for treatment-resistant schizophrenia.

Most effective for reducing suicidal thoughts.

Requires regular blood monitoring due to the risk of low white blood cell count.

Mood Stabilizers (for Schizoaffective Disorder - Bipolar Type)

Lithium, Valproate (Depakote), Lamotrigine (Lamictal).

Help control mania, mood swings, and impulsivity.

Antidepressants (for Schizoaffective Disorder - Depressive Type)

SSRIs (e.g., Fluoxetine, Sertraline) are sometimes prescribed alongside an antipsychotic.

Not recommended as a standalone treatment, as they can sometimes worsen psychosis.

2. Psychotherapy: Learning to Manage the Illness

Medication treats symptoms, but therapy helps with coping strategies, self-awareness, and daily functioning.

Cognitive Behavioral Therapy (CBT)

Helps individuals challenge delusions and hallucinations.

Teaches coping skills for anxiety and paranoia.

Focuses on realistic thinking and managing emotions.

Cognitive Remediation Therapy

Exercises to improve memory, problem-solving, and attention.

Helps with "brain fog" and cognitive deficits common in schizophrenia.

Supportive Therapy & Counseling

Encourages self-care, medication adherence, and social skills.

Family therapy can help educate loved ones about the disorder.

3. Lifestyle Changes and Holistic Approaches

Social Support & Peer Groups

NAMI (National Alliance on Mental Illness) and other organizations offer peer support groups.

Talking to others with similar experiences reduces isolation and stigma.

Diet and Nutrition

Omega-3 fatty acids (found in fish, flaxseeds) may improve brain function.

Reducing sugar and processed foods can help stabilize mood and energy levels.

Exercise and Movement

Walking, yoga, and light cardio can reduce stress and improve cognition.

Some studies suggest that regular exercise boosts dopamine levels naturally.

Sleep Hygiene

Schizophrenia often disrupts sleep patterns.

Creating a routine, avoiding caffeine late in the day, and using medication (if needed) can help.

Avoiding Substance Abuse

Drugs and alcohol worsen psychotic symptoms and interfere with medication.

Many treatment centers offer dual diagnosis programs for people with schizophrenia and addiction.

Alternative Treatments: Do They Work?

Mindfulness and Meditation → Can help with stress reduction and emotional regulation.

Music and Art Therapy → Provides an outlet for expression and emotional healing.

Vitamin D and B12 Supplements → May help improve mood and cognitive function, but not a replacement for medication.

Real-Life Case Study: Emma's Recovery Journey

Emma was diagnosed with schizoaffective disorder at 24 after experiencing severe paranoia and depressive episodes. Initially, she refused medication because she didn't believe she was sick.

After a psychotic episode that led to hospitalization, she agreed to try Risperidone and therapy. Over time, she noticed her hallucinations decreased, and her mood stabilized.

With support from her therapist, family, and a peer support group, Emma was able to return to college part-time. While she still experiences occasional symptoms, she has learned how to manage them and live a fulfilling life.

Conclusion: A Personalized Approach

Schizophrenia and schizoaffective disorder require long-term management, but with the right treatment plan, many people lead stable and fulfilling lives. The key is early intervention, consistent medication, therapy, and strong support systems.

Key Takeaways

 Schizophrenia requires two or more core symptoms for at least six months for diagnosis.
 Schizoaffective disorder includes mood symptoms alongside psychotic symptoms.
 Medication is essential for managing symptoms, but therapy helps with coping strategies.
 Lifestyle changes and social support improve overall quality of life.
 Recovery is possible with the right treatment plan.

Chapter 4

Living with Schizophrenia and Schizoaffective Disorder

Introduction

Being diagnosed with schizophrenia or schizoaffective disorder can feel overwhelming, but many people live fulfilling lives with the right treatment and support. Managing daily life requires consistency, self-awareness, and a strong support system. This chapter will explore:

Daily challenges and how to manage them

Building routines and maintaining self-care

Navigating relationships, work, and social life

Coping with stigma and advocating for yourself

Managing Daily Life with Schizophrenia or Schizoaffective Disorder

1. Creating a Routine for Stability

People with schizophrenia or schizoaffective disorder often struggle with disorganization, forgetfulness, and low motivation. Establishing a daily routine can help maintain stability.

Set a schedule: Having regular wake-up and sleep times helps regulate mood and energy.

Plan meals: Eating healthy, balanced meals prevents energy crashes.

Use reminders: Sticky notes, phone alarms, or apps can help remember appointments and medications.

Break tasks into small steps: Instead of "cleaning the house," start with "washing dishes" or "folding clothes."

Example Routine:

Time	Activity
8:00 AM	Wake up, take medication
9:00 AM	Breakfast, light exercise
11:00 AM	Therapy session or work
1:00 PM	Lunch, social activity
3:00 PM	Rest or quiet time
6:00 PM	Dinner, take evening meds
9:00 PM	Relaxation, read or watch TV
10:30 PM	Sleep

2. Managing Symptoms in Daily Life

Even with treatment, some symptoms may still occur. Learning to identify early warning signs can help prevent relapses.

Hallucinations & Delusions

Reality-checking: If you hear or see something unusual, ask a trusted person if it's real.

Distraction techniques: Listening to music, humming, or focusing on another activity can help ignore hallucinations.

Grounding exercises: Use your five senses—touch something cold, smell a strong scent, or focus on deep breathing.

Disorganized Thinking & Memory Issues

Keep a planner or journal to track thoughts and appointments.

Use checklists for daily tasks like taking medication or grocery shopping.

Ask for help when feeling overwhelmed.

Mood Symptoms (For Schizoaffective Disorder)

Track mood changes in a journal or app.

Practice mindfulness to regulate emotions.

Engage in physical activity to stabilize mood swings.

Anxiety & Paranoia

Stay in well-lit, familiar environments to reduce fear.

Limit news and social media if it increases paranoia.

Use relaxation techniques, such as deep breathing or progressive muscle relaxation.

Maintaining Physical and Mental Health

1. Medication Adherence

Not taking medication consistently is a major reason for relapse and hospitalization. Here's how to stay on track:

Set alarms or use a pill organizer to remember doses.

Ask about long-acting injections if remembering daily medication is difficult.

Talk to your doctor about side effects—adjustments can be made if needed.

2. Sleep and Rest

Sleep disturbances are common but essential for brain function. To improve sleep:

Keep a bedtime routine (dim lights, no screens before bed).

Use white noise or relaxation sounds if experiencing auditory hallucinations.

Avoid caffeine or alcohol in the evening.

3. Exercise and Nutrition

Schizophrenia medications can cause weight gain and metabolic issues, so:

Eat whole foods (lean proteins, vegetables, whole grains).

Stay hydrated and limit sugary drinks.

Do gentle movement daily (walking, yoga, stretching).

Navigating Relationships and Social Life

1. Family and Friends

Many people with schizophrenia struggle with isolation and communication. It's important to:

Educate loved ones about the disorder to reduce misunderstandings.

Set boundaries to protect your mental health.

Join support groups (NAMI, Hearing Voices Network) for connection.

2. Romantic Relationships

Dating with schizophrenia is possible but requires:

Honest conversations about symptoms and treatment.

Self-care and independence to prevent codependency.

Choosing partners who are understanding and supportive.

3. Work and Education

Many people with schizophrenia can work or go to school with the right accommodations:

Start with part-time or volunteer work to ease into employment.

Request accommodations (extra breaks, a quiet workspace, written instructions).

Consider remote work if social interactions are overwhelming.

Coping with Stigma and Self-Advocacy

1. Facing Stigma

Educate others about schizophrenia to challenge misconceptions.

Connect with supportive communities that understand your experience.

Practice self-compassion—having a mental illness is not your fault.

2. Advocating for Yourself

Be clear about your needs when talking to doctors or employers.

Know your rights—laws like the ADA protect people with mental illnesses.

Don't be afraid to change therapists or doctors if you're not receiving good care.

Real-Life Story: Mark's Journey to Stability

Mark was diagnosed with schizophrenia at 22 after experiencing paranoia and auditory hallucinations. For years, he struggled with medication noncompliance, leading to frequent hospitalizations.

With the support of his psychiatrist and family, Mark switched to a long-acting injection, which helped him stay stable. He learned coping strategies for paranoia and joined a peer support group.

Today, Mark works part-time in a bookstore and lives independently. He still has some challenges, but he has built a life where he feels in control of his illness rather than controlled by it.

Conclusion: Building a Life Beyond the Diagnosis

Living with schizophrenia or schizoaffective disorder requires commitment, support, and patience, but recovery is possible.

Key Takeaways

A structured routine helps manage daily life.
Recognizing early warning signs can prevent relapse.
Strong relationships and support networks improve mental health.
Work and education are possible with the right accommodations.
Advocating for yourself ensures better care and treatment.

Chapter 5

Supporting a Loved One with Schizophrenia or Schizoaffective Disorder

Introduction

Supporting a loved one with schizophrenia or schizoaffective disorder can be challenging and emotionally draining, but your role is crucial in their recovery. This chapter will cover:

Understanding their experience and struggles

Providing emotional and practical support

Setting boundaries without guilt

Helping them manage treatment and crises

Taking care of yourself as a caregiver

Understanding What Your Loved One is Going Through

1. Common Symptoms and Their Impact

Schizophrenia and schizoaffective disorder cause symptoms that affect thinking, emotions, and behavior. It's important to recognize what they might be experiencing:

Positive Symptoms (Added Experiences)

Hallucinations: Seeing, hearing, or feeling things that aren't real.
Delusions: Strong, false beliefs that don't change even with evidence.
Disorganized thinking: Trouble keeping thoughts straight or expressing ideas clearly.

Negative Symptoms (Lost Abilities)

Emotional flatness: Lack of facial expressions or enthusiasm.
Social withdrawal: Avoiding family and friends.
Lack of motivation: Difficulty completing daily tasks.

Cognitive Symptoms

Memory problems: Forgetting things or struggling to focus.
Poor decision-making: Impulsive or irrational choices.

Mood Symptoms (Schizoaffective Disorder Only)

Depression: Feeling hopeless, unmotivated, or numb.
Mania: High energy, impulsiveness, or reckless behavior.

Understanding that these symptoms are not intentional can help you respond with patience and empathy.

How to Support Your Loved One

1. Communicating with Empathy

Many people with schizophrenia feel misunderstood or dismissed. Use these strategies to communicate effectively:

Be patient: Processing thoughts takes time. Let them express themselves at their own pace.

Use clear, simple language: Avoid abstract or complicated conversations. Validate their emotions: Instead of dismissing their feelings, acknowledge them. Example:

Unhelpful: "You're being paranoid. That's not real."

Helpful: "I can see that you're really scared. That must be hard for you." Don't argue about delusions: Instead, focus on how they feel rather than proving them wrong.

Example of a Supportive Conversation

Wrong Approach:

"You're just imagining things. You're fine."
Better Approach:

"I know that must feel real to you. Do you want to talk about it?"

2. Encouraging Treatment Without Forcing It

Many people with schizophrenia resist treatment due to paranoia, lack of insight, or side effects. Here's how to support them without pushing too hard:

Frame treatment as a way to feel better, not as a "cure."
Offer to attend doctor's appointments with them.
Respect their autonomy—forcing treatment often backfires.
If they refuse medication, explore alternatives (therapy, lifestyle changes).

What if They Don't Believe They're Ill? (Anosognosia)

Some people with schizophrenia have anosognosia, meaning they don't recognize their illness.

Instead of saying, "You need meds because you're sick," try:

"I've noticed you've been struggling. Do you think there's something that could help?"

Offer small compromises: "Can we try this for a week and see how you feel?"

3. Managing Crisis Situations

Crises can be scary and unpredictable. Knowing what to do can prevent harm and de-escalate situations.

Signs of a Crisis:

Increased paranoia or aggression
Talking about suicide or self-harm
Refusing food, water, or medication
Becoming extremely confused or unresponsive

How to De-escalate a Crisis:

Stay calm—your energy affects theirs.
Speak softly and avoid sudden movements.
Give them space and avoid crowding them.
Don't argue or criticize—focus on helping.

When to Call for Help

🚑 If they are a danger to themselves or others, call emergency services.

Explain the situation: "My loved one has schizophrenia and is in crisis. They need psychiatric help."

Ask for a mental health crisis team instead of police, if possible.

Setting Boundaries Without Guilt

Supporting someone doesn't mean sacrificing your own well-being. Boundaries protect both you and them.

Be clear about what you can and cannot do.
 It's okay to say no if their demands are unreasonable.
 Encourage independence instead of enabling.

Examples of Healthy Boundaries:

Unhealthy: "I'll drop everything whenever you call."
Healthy: "I care about you, but I can't always answer immediately. Let's set a time to check in."

Unhealthy: "You can live here rent-free forever."
Healthy: "You can stay here for three months while we work on a housing plan."

Setting boundaries isn't selfish—it helps both of you thrive.

Taking Care of Yourself as a Caregiver

1. Preventing Burnout

Caring for someone with schizophrenia is emotionally exhausting. You need to recharge to be a good supporter.
Join a support group (NAMI, family support groups).

Take breaks—you don't have to be available 24/7.
Prioritize self-care (exercise, hobbies, therapy).

2. Finding Your Own Support System

You are not alone. Connect with others who understand:

Online forums (Reddit, Facebook groups)

Local caregiver support groups

Therapists specializing in caregiver stress

Real-Life Story: Lisa's Journey as a Caregiver

Lisa's younger brother, Jake, was diagnosed with schizoaffective disorder at 19. At first, Lisa felt helpless and frustrated because Jake refused treatment and often talked to unseen people.

Through a family support group, she learned how to communicate without judgment and set boundaries. Over time, Jake agreed to try therapy and a low-dose medication. He still has challenges, but their relationship has improved, and Lisa no longer feels like she has to "fix" everything alone.

Lisa's advice: "You can't force recovery, but you can be a steady presence. Take care of yourself too."

Conclusion: You're Making a Difference

Supporting a loved one with schizophrenia or schizoaffective disorder is one of the hardest yet most meaningful things you can do.

Key Takeaways:

Empathy and patience go a long way.

Encouraging treatment without forcing it is key.
Crisis planning can prevent harm.
Setting boundaries protects your mental health.
You deserve support too—reach out for help.

Chapter 6

Medications and Treatments for Schizophrenia and Schizoaffective Disorder

Introduction

Medication and therapy are the foundation of treatment for schizophrenia and schizoaffective disorder. While some people resist medication due to side effects or distrust, understanding how these treatments work, their benefits, and how to manage side effects can help individuals stay committed to their care.

This chapter will cover:

✓ Antipsychotic medications—how they work and their side effects

✓ Mood stabilizers and antidepressants for schizoaffective disorder

✓ Psychotherapy and non-medication treatments

✓ Managing medication side effects

✓ How to encourage treatment adherence

1. Antipsychotic Medications: The Core of Treatment

Antipsychotic medications are the primary treatment for schizophrenia and schizoaffective disorder. They help reduce hallucinations, delusions, and disorganized thinking.

Types of Antipsychotics

1. First-Generation (Typical) Antipsychotics

Older medications that are effective but cause more movement-related side effects.

Examples: Haloperidol (Haldol), Chlorpromazine (Thorazine), Fluphenazine

Pros: Strong at reducing hallucinations and delusions

Cons: More likely to cause tremors, stiffness, and involuntary movements (extrapyramidal symptoms)

2. Second-Generation (Atypical) Antipsychotics

Newer medications that have fewer movement-related side effects but may cause weight gain and metabolic issues.

Examples: Risperidone (Risperdal), Olanzapine (Zyprexa), Quetiapine (Seroquel), Aripiprazole (Abilify)

Pros: Fewer motor side effects, sometimes help with mood symptoms

Cons: Higher risk of weight gain, diabetes, and sedation

3. Long-Acting Injectable Antipsychotics (LAIs)

For individuals who struggle with daily medication, long-acting injections (LAIs) provide weeks of coverage in a single shot.

Examples: Paliperidone (Invega Sustenna), Aripiprazole (Abilify Maintena), Risperidone (Risperdal Consta)

Pros: Helps with medication adherence, fewer daily struggles

Cons: Requires doctor visits for injections

✓ Which one is best? It depends on individual symptoms, side effect tolerance, and lifestyle.

2. Mood Stabilizers and Antidepressants for Schizoaffective Disorder

Schizoaffective disorder includes mood symptoms, so additional medications are often needed.

1. Mood Stabilizers (for Bipolar-Type Schizoaffective Disorder)

Lithium: Prevents manic and depressive episodes but requires blood monitoring.

Valproate (Depakote): Helps with mania but can cause weight gain.

Lamotrigine (Lamictal): Better for depression than mania.

2. Antidepressants (for Depressive-Type Schizoaffective Disorder)

SSRIs (e.g., Sertraline, Fluoxetine, Escitalopram): Help with depression and anxiety.

Bupropion (Wellbutrin): Less risk of weight gain but can increase anxiety.

💡 Important: Antidepressants alone can trigger psychosis in some people. They should only be taken with an antipsychotic in schizoaffective disorder.

3. Psychotherapy and Non-Medication Treatments

While medication is essential, therapy and lifestyle changes play a key role in long-term recovery.

1. Cognitive Behavioral Therapy for Psychosis (CBTp)

✓ Helps people challenge delusions and cope with hallucinations

✓ Improves problem-solving and emotional regulation

✓ Can be done individually or in groups

2. Family Therapy and Psychoeducation

✓ Helps families understand the illness and improve communication

✓ Reduces stress and relapses

3. Social Skills Training

✓ Teaches how to navigate social situations

✓ Helps with building friendships and finding jobs

4. Peer Support and Support Groups

✓ Connects individuals with others who understand their struggles

✓ Reduces isolation and stigma

4. Managing Medication Side Effects

Many people stop taking medications due to side effects, so knowing how to manage them is crucial.

1. Weight Gain & Metabolic Issues

Common with: Olanzapine, Quetiapine, Clozapine

Solutions:

✓ Healthy diet and exercise

✓ Metformin (a diabetes medication that helps with weight gain)

2. Sedation & Fatigue

Common with: Quetiapine, Clozapine, Olanzapine

Solutions:

✓ Take medication at night

✓ Consider switching to a less sedating option (e.g., Aripiprazole)

3. Tremors & Stiffness (Extrapyramidal Symptoms)

Common with: Haloperidol, Risperidone

Solutions:

✓ Lower the dose

✓ Use medications like Benztropine (Cogentin) or Diphenhydramine

4. Sexual Dysfunction

Common with: Risperidone, Haloperidol

Solutions:

✓ Talk to a doctor about adjusting the dose or switching medications

5. How to Encourage Medication Adherence

Many people with schizophrenia or schizoaffective disorder stop taking their medication due to side effects, lack of insight, or stigma.

✔ Frame medication as a way to feel better, not as a punishment

✔ Use reminders or pill organizers to avoid missed doses

✔ Consider long-acting injectables if daily pills are a struggle

✔ Encourage open discussions about side effects rather than stopping suddenly

✔ Work with a doctor to find the best balance between symptom control and side effects

Real-Life Story: David's Journey with Medication

David, a 27-year-old with schizophrenia, hated taking his medication because it made him feel "foggy." He often skipped doses, leading to a relapse that landed him in the hospital.

His psychiatrist switched him to a long-acting injectable, which helped stabilize him without daily pills. David also started therapy to process his paranoia. Today, he accepts that medication is part of his wellness and actively participates in his treatment.

David's advice: "It's okay to hate medication, but it helps me live my life. Find the right one for you."

Conclusion: Finding the Right Treatment Plan

✓ Antipsychotics are the foundation of treatment for schizophrenia and schizoaffective disorder.

✓ Mood stabilizers and antidepressants help manage mood symptoms in schizoaffective disorder.

✓ Therapy and social support improve recovery and coping.

✓ Managing side effects is crucial to sticking with treatment.

✓ Encouraging medication adherence without force is key.

Chapter 7

Daily Life with Schizophrenia and Schizoaffective Disorder

Introduction

Living with schizophrenia or schizoaffective disorder presents unique challenges, but structure, support, and coping strategies can make daily life manageable. This chapter will explore:

✔ Creating a stable daily routine

✔ Handling work, school, and relationships

✔ Coping with symptoms in everyday situations

✔ The role of family and caregivers

✔ Developing independence and self-care

1. Creating a Stable Daily Routine

Schizophrenia and schizoaffective disorder can make time management and motivation difficult. A stable routine helps improve mental clarity and reduce stress.

Steps to Build a Routine

✔ Set consistent wake-up and bedtime hours – Sleep is crucial for symptom control.

✔ Schedule medication times – Set reminders or use a pill organizer.

✔ Plan meals – Eating regularly stabilizes energy and mood.

✔ Include activities that bring joy – Reading, music, or light exercise can improve well-being.

✔ Break tasks into small steps – Instead of "clean the house," try "wash dishes for 5 minutes."

💡 Pro Tip: Using a planner or app can help track important tasks and medication schedules.

2. Managing Work, School, and Responsibilities

Work and Schizophrenia/Schizoaffective Disorder

Many people with schizophrenia can work, but job choice matters. Some people thrive in structured, low-stress environments, while others prefer flexible or part-time jobs.

✔ Best jobs for symptom management:

Library assistant (quiet environment)

Data entry (structured and repetitive)

Gardening or outdoor jobs (low social interaction)

Creative work (painting, music, writing)

💡 If full-time work is overwhelming, consider part-time, freelance, or supported employment programs.

School and Education

For students, accommodations like extra test time, note-taking help, or online courses can make education more manageable. Schools often offer disability support services to assist.

3. Coping with Symptoms in Daily Life

Even with treatment, symptoms can flare up due to stress, lack of sleep, or medication changes.

Handling Hallucinations

✓ Distract yourself – Listen to music, read, or do an activity.

✓ Reality-check with someone you trust – Ask, "Do you hear that too?"

✓ Use grounding techniques – Focus on your surroundings and engage your senses.

Dealing with Delusions and Paranoia

✓ Avoid arguments – Instead of saying, "That's not real," try, "I understand why that feels real to you."

✓ Reduce stress – High anxiety can make delusions stronger.

✓ Keep a journal – Writing thoughts down helps track patterns and reality-check.

Handling Disorganized Thinking

✔ Use notes and reminders – A whiteboard or phone app can help with forgetfulness.

✔ Slow down – Break thoughts into smaller parts and ask others to repeat information if needed.

✔ Practice deep breathing – Helps with mental fog and focus.

4. Relationships and Social Life

Social connections improve mental health, but schizophrenia can make relationships challenging due to withdrawal, paranoia, or communication difficulties.

Tips for Friendships

✔ Start small – Texting or online groups can be easier than face-to-face meetings.

✔ Be honest – Saying, "I sometimes struggle with conversations, but I enjoy your company," can help.

✔ Join supportive communities – NAMI (National Alliance on Mental Illness) or local support groups can help.

Dating and Romantic Relationships

✔ Honesty matters – Some people prefer to disclose their condition early, others wait until trust is built.

✔ Healthy relationships require balance – Your needs matter just as much as your partner's.

✓ Look for understanding partners – Someone who respects mental health challenges is key.

💡 Pro Tip: If a relationship is causing stress or worsening symptoms, it might not be healthy.

5. The Role of Family and Caregivers

Family members and caregivers play a huge role in support. However, misunderstandings can happen, so education is important.

What Families Can Do

✓ Learn about schizophrenia – The more they understand, the more supportive they can be.

✓ Avoid blame – Schizophrenia is a medical condition, not a choice.

✓ Encourage treatment without force – Saying, "I want to help you feel better," is better than "You need to take your meds."

Setting Boundaries

Family support is valuable, but boundaries are needed to avoid caregiver burnout.

✓ Schedule breaks for caregivers – Everyone needs self-care.

✓ Encourage independence – Small tasks (like making meals) build confidence.

✓ Use support services – Respite care or therapy can help families manage stress.

6. Developing Independence and Self-Care

Many people with schizophrenia live independently with the right support.

✓ Supported Housing Programs – Some cities offer housing with mental health support on-site.

✓ Grocery and meal planning – Having simple meal options can prevent skipping meals.

✓ Budgeting help – Using cash envelopes or financial apps can track spending.

✓ Public transport or rideshare apps – Helps with mobility if driving is not an option.

💡 Independence is built over time. Small steps lead to big confidence.

Real-Life Story: Emily's Journey to Stability

Emily was diagnosed with schizoaffective disorder at 22. She struggled with paranoia, lost jobs due to disorganization, and had difficulty maintaining friendships.

Through therapy, she learned time management skills and found a supportive employer who allowed her to take breaks when needed. Emily also joined an online support group, which helped her feel less alone.

Today, Emily lives independently, works part-time, and manages her symptoms with a mix of medication, therapy, and structure. Her advice:

"It's not about being perfect—it's about finding what works for you."

Conclusion: Building a Meaningful Life

✔ Daily structure helps maintain stability.

✔ Work and school are possible with the right accommodations.

✔ Managing symptoms takes practice and support.

✔ Relationships require patience and understanding.

✔ Independence is possible with small steps.

Chapter 8

Crisis Management – Handling Psychotic Episodes and Hospitalization

Introduction

Psychotic episodes and crises can be overwhelming for both individuals with schizophrenia or schizoaffective disorder and their loved ones. However, recognizing early warning signs and having a crisis plan can prevent hospitalizations or make them less distressing.

This chapter will cover:

✓ Understanding psychotic episodes

✓ Early warning signs of relapse

✓ Crisis planning and de-escalation strategies

✓ When hospitalization is necessary

✓ What to expect during and after hospitalization

1. Understanding Psychotic Episodes

A psychotic episode is when a person loses touch with reality, experiencing hallucinations, delusions, paranoia, or severe disorganization. These episodes can last for hours, days, or even weeks, depending on treatment and intervention.

Common Triggers for Psychotic Episodes

✓ Stopping medication suddenly

✓ Extreme stress or trauma

✓ Sleep deprivation

✓ Drug or alcohol use

✓ Major life changes (moving, job loss, relationship stress)

✓ Illness or physical health problems

💡 Not all episodes are the same. Some may involve only mild paranoia, while others can include full delusions or disorganized behavior.

2. Early Warning Signs of Relapse

Catching symptoms early can help prevent a full-blown episode. Some common warning signs include:

✓ Increased paranoia or suspicion

✓ Changes in speech – more disorganized or harder to follow

✓ Hearing voices more often or seeing things that aren't there

✓ Withdrawing from family and friends

✓ Neglecting self-care – not showering, eating, or cleaning

✓ Sudden changes in sleep – sleeping too much or too little

✓ Speaking about bizarre ideas or feeling watched

✓ Increased irritability, anger, or fear without a clear reason

💡 Keeping a symptom journal can help track patterns and notice warning signs sooner.

3. Crisis Planning and De-Escalation Strategies

Creating a Crisis Plan

A crisis plan should be written down and shared with trusted people. It includes:

✓ Emergency contacts – Family, close friends, or mental health professionals

✓ List of triggers – To help prevent future episodes

✓ Medications and dosage information

✓ Preferred hospital or treatment center

✓ Comforting strategies – Music, specific foods, grounding techniques

✓ Safety measures – What to do if self-harm or aggression occurs

💡 Having a plan can reduce panic and confusion during a crisis.

How to De-Escalate a Psychotic Episode

If a loved one is experiencing psychosis, the goal is to keep them calm and prevent harm.

✓ Stay calm – Speak slowly and softly. Avoid shouting.

✓ Validate feelings – Say, "I understand this is scary for you."

✓ Avoid arguing about delusions – Instead of "That's not real," try "I see that this feels real to you."

✓ Create a safe space – Remove loud noises, bright lights, and stressful stimuli.

✓ Encourage hydration and food – Dehydration or hunger can make symptoms worse.

✓ Suggest medication (if applicable) – If they have skipped doses, encourage them to take it.

💡 If the situation is dangerous, don't hesitate to seek emergency help.

4. When Hospitalization is Necessary

Hospitalization is sometimes needed if someone is a danger to themselves or others, or if symptoms are too severe to manage at home.

✓ Signs hospitalization may be needed:

Severe delusions (believing they are in danger, or that they must harm themselves/others)

Not eating, drinking, or sleeping for days

Extreme aggression or violence

Unable to care for themselves at all

Severe suicidal thoughts or self-harm

💡 Voluntary vs. Involuntary Hospitalization:
✓ If the person agrees to go, voluntary hospitalization is smoother and allows them to participate in their care.

✔ If they refuse but are in danger, an involuntary hold (such as a 72-hour psychiatric hold) may be required.

5. What to Expect During and After Hospitalization

During Hospitalization

✔ Medication adjustments – Doctors may change or adjust medications.

✔ Psychiatric evaluations – A team will assess symptoms and progress.

✔ Therapy sessions – Some hospitals offer group or individual therapy.

✔ Limited phone use – Many psychiatric units restrict devices for safety.

✔ Structured routine – Meals, medication, and activities happen on a schedule.

💡 Hospitals are NOT like in the movies. They are usually calm, controlled environments focused on treatment.

After Hospitalization: The Recovery Process

Leaving the hospital doesn't mean symptoms are gone—it means they are more manageable.

✔ Follow up with doctors – Adjustments to medication may still be needed.

✔ Continue therapy – Cognitive Behavioral Therapy (CBT) or family therapy can help.

✔ Ease back into daily life – Rushing back into work/school can cause stress.

✔ Check in with loved ones – Having support prevents relapse.

✔ Stick to a routine – Stability reduces symptom flare-ups.

💡 The first few weeks after a hospital stay are critical—extra support is needed.

Real-Life Story: James' Experience with Crisis and Recovery

James, a 27-year-old with schizoaffective disorder, was doing well on medication. However, stress from losing his job made him stop taking his meds, thinking he didn't need them anymore.

Slowly, he started hearing voices again, became paranoid about his neighbors, and believed his food was poisoned. One day, he walked into traffic, convinced he was invincible. His sister got him to the hospital, where he stayed for two weeks.

At first, James was angry about being hospitalized. But with medication, therapy, and support, he stabilized and learned the importance of sticking to treatment.

Today, he keeps a crisis plan, checks in with his psychiatrist monthly, and uses stress-management techniques to prevent future episodes.

His advice: "Never be ashamed of needing help. Getting help saved my life."

Conclusion: Preparation Can Save Lives

✔ Recognizing early warning signs can prevent full psychotic episodes.

✓ A crisis plan helps everyone stay prepared.

✓ De-escalation strategies can keep situations calm and safe.

✓ Hospitalization is sometimes necessary but is not a failure—it's a tool for recovery.

✓ The weeks after hospitalization are critical for long-term stability.

Chapter 9

Medication and Treatment Options – Finding the Right Balance

Introduction

Managing schizophrenia or schizoaffective disorder often requires a combination of medication, therapy, and lifestyle adjustments. Medications, particularly antipsychotics, play a crucial role in reducing symptoms like hallucinations, delusions, and disorganized thinking. However, side effects and individual responses vary, making finding the right treatment plan a process of trial and adjustment.

This chapter will cover:

✓ Types of medications for schizophrenia and schizoaffective disorder

✓ How antipsychotics work

✓ Common side effects and how to manage them

✓ Therapies and non-medication treatments

✓ Alternative and complementary treatments

1. Types of Medications for Schizophrenia and Schizoaffective Disorder

The main type of medication used is antipsychotics, which help regulate dopamine and serotonin levels in the brain.

First-Generation (Typical) Antipsychotics

✓ Developed in the 1950s

✓ Reduce hallucinations, delusions, and paranoia

✓ Higher risk of movement-related side effects

Common first-generation antipsychotics:

Haloperidol (Haldol)

Chlorpromazine (Thorazine)

Fluphenazine (Prolixin)

Perphenazine (Trilafon)

💡 Pros: Very effective for psychosis
💡 Cons: High risk of tardive dyskinesia (involuntary movements)

Second-Generation (Atypical) Antipsychotics

✓ Developed in the 1990s and later

✓ Treat hallucinations, delusions, mood symptoms, and cognitive issues

✓ Lower risk of movement-related side effects but higher metabolic risks

Common second-generation antipsychotics:

Risperidone (Risperdal)

Olanzapine (Zyprexa)

Quetiapine (Seroquel)

Aripiprazole (Abilify)

Clozapine (Clozaril) – used for treatment-resistant schizophrenia

💡 Pros: Fewer movement-related side effects
💡 Cons: Can cause weight gain, diabetes, and drowsiness

Mood Stabilizers and Antidepressants

People with schizoaffective disorder (especially the bipolar type) may also take:

✔ Mood stabilizers – Lithium, valproate (Depakote), or lamotrigine

(Lamictal)

✔ Antidepressants – SSRIs like fluoxetine (Prozac) or sertraline (Zoloft)

2. How Antipsychotics Work

Antipsychotic medications work by balancing neurotransmitters in the brain, mainly:

✔ Dopamine – Too much dopamine is linked to hallucinations and

delusions

✔ Serotonin – Plays a role in mood and cognitive functions

✔ Glutamate – Important for memory and thinking

💡 Antipsychotics don't cure schizophrenia, but they help manage symptoms and improve quality of life.

3. Common Side Effects and How to Manage Them

Like all medications, antipsychotics come with side effects. Here's how to handle them:

💡 Always report side effects to a doctor—medication changes or dose adjustments can help.

4. Therapies and Non-Medication Treatments

While medication is crucial, therapy and lifestyle changes also play a major role in managing schizophrenia and schizoaffective disorder.

Cognitive Behavioral Therapy (CBT)

✓ Helps challenge delusions and paranoia

✓ Teaches coping strategies for hallucinations

✓ Supports problem-solving and emotional regulation

💡 Example: Learning to question a delusion by asking, "Is there concrete evidence for this?"

Cognitive Remediation Therapy (CRT)

✓ Improves memory, attention, and problem-solving skills

✓ Helps manage disorganized thinking

💡 Example: Using puzzles, memory exercises, and structured thinking tasks.

Social Skills Training (SST)

✓ Improves communication and relationship-building

✓ Helps navigate conversations and body language

✓ Reduces social anxiety

💡 Example: Practicing eye contact and small talk in therapy sessions.

Family Therapy & Psychoeducation

✓ Educates family members about schizophrenia

✓ Improves communication within the family

✓ Reduces stress and improves support systems

💡 Example: Teaching family how to respond to symptoms without worsening paranoia.

5. Alternative and Complementary Treatments

Many people find non-medication treatments helpful alongside traditional care.

Lifestyle Changes

✓ Regular sleep schedule – Prevents worsening of symptoms

✓ Balanced diet – Supports brain health and reduces metabolic risks

✓ Exercise – Boosts mood and cognitive function

✓ Avoiding drugs and alcohol – Reduces psychosis risk

Mindfulness & Meditation

✓ Helps reduce stress and paranoia

✓ Can improve focus and emotional control

💡 Example: Practicing deep breathing when feeling anxious.

Art & Music Therapy

✓ Provides emotional expression and stress relief

✓ Can reduce anxiety and improve social skills

💡 Example: Playing an instrument or painting to express emotions.

Nutritional Supplements

✓ Omega-3 fatty acids – May support brain function

✓ Vitamin D & B vitamins – Can help with mood regulation

✓ NAC (N-Acetylcysteine) – Shows potential in reducing symptoms

💡 Always consult a doctor before taking supplements.

Real-Life Story: Maria's Journey to Finding the Right Medication

Maria, a 30-year-old woman with schizoaffective disorder, struggled with hallucinations and mood swings. Her first antipsychotic, Risperidone, helped but caused significant weight gain.

With her psychiatrist, she switched to Aripiprazole (Abilify), which had fewer metabolic side effects. She also started CBT therapy and exercise, which helped her manage paranoia and mood fluctuations.

Now, Maria has a balanced treatment plan:

✔ Medication that works for her

✔ Regular therapy sessions

✔ Healthy routines and lifestyle changes

Her advice: "Finding the right medication takes time, but once you do, life becomes more manageable."

Conclusion: A Holistic Approach to Treatment

✔ Medication is the foundation of treatment, but it's not the only tool.

✔ Managing side effects is important for long-term success.

✔ Therapies like CBT and social skills training improve daily functioning.

✔ Lifestyle changes, mindfulness, and alternative treatments can complement medical care.

✔ Every person responds differently—finding the right treatment plan is a journey.

Chapter 10

Long-Term Management & Recovery Building a Stable and Fulfilling Life

Introduction

Schizophrenia and schizoaffective disorder are chronic conditions, but that doesn't mean a fulfilling, meaningful life isn't possible. Many people successfully manage their symptoms, maintain relationships, work, and find joy in everyday life. Long-term management is about stability, consistency, and learning how to navigate challenges without losing progress.

In this chapter, we'll discuss:

✔ How to maintain stability over time

✔ Relapse prevention strategies

✔ Building a strong support network

✔ Navigating work, relationships, and personal goals

✔ Finding hope and meaning in life

1. Maintaining Stability Over Time

Managing schizophrenia or schizoaffective disorder is like running a marathon, not a sprint. Small, consistent actions help build long-term stability.

The Keys to Stability:

✔ Medication adherence – Taking medication regularly as prescribed

✔ Routine and structure – Having a predictable daily schedule

✔ Stress management – Reducing triggers that worsen symptoms

✔ Healthy sleep habits – Getting enough rest for brain function

✔ Regular therapy or check-ins – Talking to a professional, even when feeling okay

💡 Example: Maria, who has schizoaffective disorder, keeps a daily routine that includes taking medication at the same time, eating balanced meals, exercising, and practicing meditation before bed.

2. Relapse Prevention Strategies

A relapse happens when symptoms return or worsen after a period of stability. Recognizing early warning signs can help prevent a full-blown relapse.

Common Early Warning Signs of Relapse:

✔ Feeling overwhelmed, anxious, or more withdrawn

✔ Changes in sleep patterns – sleeping too much or too little

✔ Hallucinations or paranoia returning in small ways

✔ Skipping medication or feeling like you don't need it anymore

✔ Trouble concentrating, organizing thoughts, or feeling confused

💡 What to Do if You Notice Early Signs:

1. Increase self-care – Get enough sleep, eat well, and reduce stress.

2. Talk to someone – A therapist, doctor, or trusted friend.

3. Medication check – If you've skipped doses, get back on track.

4. Avoid isolating yourself – Stay connected with others.

5. Emergency plan – Have a plan in place if symptoms get worse.

⚶ Relapse Example: Alex had been stable for a year, but after missing a few doses of medication, he started feeling paranoid again. Instead of waiting, he called his psychiatrist and adjusted his medication, avoiding a full relapse.

3. Building a Strong Support Network

A support system makes a huge difference in long-term recovery. It helps to have people who understand your condition and can provide encouragement and practical help.

Types of Support Systems:

✔ Family & close friends – Educating them about your condition helps them support you.

✔ Therapists & psychiatrists – Regular check-ins prevent setbacks.

✔ Support groups – Online or in-person groups connect you with others who understand.

✔ Workplace accommodations – Employers who support mental health needs.

💡 How to Strengthen Your Support System:

✓ Educate loved ones – Teach them about your condition and what helps.

✓ Communicate needs clearly – Let people know when you need space or support.

✓ Seek new connections – If family isn't supportive, find people who are.

4. Navigating Work, Relationships, and Goals

Many people with schizophrenia or schizoaffective disorder can work, have fulfilling relationships, and pursue hobbies and interests.

Managing Work and Responsibilities:

✓ Find a job that fits your strengths – Some jobs are lower stress and have flexible hours.

✓ Request workplace accommodations – A quiet space, flexible schedule, or extra breaks may help.

✓ Balance workload – Avoid overwhelming yourself with too much responsibility.

⚖ Example: Jordan, who has schizophrenia, works part-time in graphic design. He uses noise-canceling headphones to stay focused and communicates openly with his boss about his needs.

Relationships and Social Life:

✓ Set boundaries – Avoid people who increase stress or doubt your experiences.

✔ Be open about your condition (when comfortable) – It helps others understand.

✔ Engage in hobbies and interests – Doing things you enjoy brings purpose.

⬧ Example: Emily, who has schizoaffective disorder, joined a book club. She found friends who don't judge her, and it helped reduce her isolation.

Setting and Achieving Personal Goals:

✔ Start small – Break big goals into smaller steps.

✔ Use tools like planners and reminders – Helps with organization.

✔ Celebrate small wins – Progress, no matter how small, is worth acknowledging.

5. Finding Hope and Meaning in Life

Recovery isn't just about managing symptoms—it's about finding meaning and joy in life.

Ways to Build a Meaningful Life:

✔ Helping others – Volunteering, mentoring, or supporting peers.

✔ Creative expression – Writing, art, or music can be therapeutic.

✔ Spirituality or mindfulness – Some find comfort in meditation, religion, or philosophy.

✔ Self-acceptance – Knowing you are more than your diagnosis.

⚚ Real-Life Story: David, a man living with schizophrenia, started writing poetry about his experiences. Sharing his work in mental health groups gave him purpose and helped others feel less alone.

💡 Key Takeaway: A fulfilling life is possible. It may look different from what you once imagined, but it can still be full of love, creativity, connection, and growth.

Conclusion: The Journey Doesn't End Here

✓ Managing schizophrenia or schizoaffective disorder is a lifelong journey, but with the right support, tools, and mindset, stability and fulfillment are possible.

✓ Relapses can happen, but they don't mean failure. Learning from setbacks makes you stronger.

✓ Surrounding yourself with supportive people and seeking help when needed makes a difference.

✓ You are more than your diagnosis—your life has value, and you deserve happiness.

Final Message: You Are Not Alone

💡 If you take away one thing from this book, let it be this:
You are not alone. There is hope, support, and a future worth fighting for.

If you or a loved one is struggling, reach out—to a doctor, therapist, support group, or friend. Recovery isn't about being "cured"—it's about learning how to live a fulfilling life despite the challenges.

Made in United States
Orlando, FL
22 April 2025

60751025R00042